ALL RIGHTS RESERVED. No part of this report may be modified or altered in any form whatsoever, electronic, or mechanical, including photocopying, recording, or by any informational storage or retrieval system without express written, dated and signed permission from the author.

AFFILIATE DISCLAIMER. The short, direct, non-legal version is this: Some of the links in this report may be affiliate links which means that I earn money if you choose to buy from that vendor at some point in the near future. I do not choose which products and services to promote based upon which pay me the most, I choose based upon my decision of which I would recommend to a dear friend. You will never pay more for an item by clicking through my affiliate link, and, in fact, may pay less since I negotiate special offers for my readers that are not available elsewhere.

DISCLAIMER AND/OR LEGAL NOTICES: The information presented herein represents the view of the author as of the date of publication. Because of the rate with which conditions change, the author reserves the right to alter and update his opinion based on the new conditions. The report is for informational purposes only. While every attempt has been made to verify the information provided in this report, neither the author nor his affiliates/partners assume any responsibility for errors, inaccuracies or omissions. Any slights of people or organizations are unintentional. If advice concerning legal or related matters is needed, the services of a fully qualified professional should be sought. This report is not intended for use as a source of legal or accounting advice. You should be aware of any laws which govern business transactions or other business practices in your country and state. Any reference to any person or business whether living or dead is purely coincidental.

Copyright © 2021

TABLE OF CONTENTS

Introduction	4
Prepare Yourself	8
Identify Your Passions and Interests	13
Validate Your Side Hustle	17
Determine What Sets You Apart From Your Competitors	21
Define Your Goals	24
Create Milestones	27
Determine How You Will Sell	31
Start Selling	35
Market Yourself	38
Get Feedback From Your Customers	42
Provide Amazing Experiences For Your Customers	45
Build Sustainable Cash Flow	48
Side Hustle Your Way To Freedom	52

> Everything you can imagine is real.

Pablo Picasso

Introduction

We all have things that we absolutely love to do. Maybe you love to write. Maybe taking photos makes you feel like a million dollars. Or maybe you love crafting hand-made signs. It's the thing that makes you feel alive. That creates a fire in your bones.

But you don't think you could ever make money from your passion. *Surely*, you think, *I can't make money doing [insert your passion]. Nobody would pay me to do that. It's too much fun and I love it too much. No way could I make money doing that.*

That's where you're wrong. Thanks to the internet, almost any passion can be turned into a profitable side hustle.

Did you catch that?

You can make money doing the things that you love the most. Yep. You can turn your passion project into a profitable project.

Let's be honest. We all could use some extra cash in our lives. We've got bills to pay, kids to send to school, car repairs to make, and a dozen other expenses. Some extra cash could be really useful and go a long way toward making our lives easier.

How would it change your life to make an extra $1,000 per month? Or double that?

You can easily make that if you know how to create a profitable side hustle. In fact, if you know what you're doing, you may be able to turn your passion project into your full-time job. Can you imagine how rewarding it would be to get to do what you love for your job? Your quality of life would drastically improve, and your overall life satisfaction would go through the roof.

Chris Guillebeau says this:

> *A side hustle isn't just about money in the bank, as helpful as that can be. A side hustle really can change your life. When you build something for yourself, even as you continue to work your day job, you*

become empowered. You gain confidence. You create security, both in the form of that extra cash and also in the fact that you're opening up future opportunities for yourself.

Of course, all this raises the critical question: how do you start a side hustle?

Because, honestly, there are a lot of questions that come with starting a side hustle.

- What products or services should you sell?
- Where should you sell them?
- How much should you charge?
- How do you market yourself?
- How do you determine if your side hustle will actually make money?

In this eBook, we're going to give you a roadmap for turning your passion into a profitable side hustle. We're going to guide you, step-by-step, to making money doing what you love. By the end, you'll know exactly what you need to do in order to start making money on your side hustle right away.

Ready? Let's get started!

> **Believe in your dreams, no matter how impossible they seem.**
>
> **Walt Disney**

Prepare Yourself

If you're interested in get rich quick schemes, then this book isn't for you. Because here's the reality: creating a profitable side hustle takes a lot of time, diligence, hard work, blood, sweat, and tears (well, hopefully not tears!).

If you want to succeed with your side hustle, prepare to put in some work. You shouldn't expect to start working and immediately have boatloads of cash pouring in. You need to be ready to put in many hours of work over the long haul.

How do you create the motivation needed to put in all that hard work?
Take a look at your life as it currently is. Are you living your best life now? Are you completely fulfilled with your day job? Are there other things you would love to do to make money? Do you see others doing what you want to do?

If you're not living your best life now, let that serve as a motivator for your side hustle. You really can make money doing what you absolutely LOVE. You can generate significant income doing something that brings great satisfaction into your life.

How would it change your life if you were doing work that actually made you happy?

How would it revolutionize things for you if you actually enjoyed the work you do every day?

To increase your motivation for your side hustle, envision what a successful outcome would look like for your side hustle. Paint a picture in your mind of what your best life will look like.

Get very clear on:

- How badly you want to succeed in your side hustle
- The benefits you'll experience
- How the extra cash will help you
- The joy you'll experience in doing what you love

If you're not highly motivated to make your side hustle a reality, it won't happen. Because here's the truth: your side hustle is going to take you away from other good things that you could be doing.

You may need to give up:

- Television
- Hobbies
- Some time with friends

You may even need to sacrifice some time with your family, although we obviously don't recommend doing this over the long haul.

The point is simply that you're going to have to make sacrifices in order to make your side hustle a reality. You're going to need to do the hard work necessary. You have to be willing to give up some good things in order to achieve a great thing.

What most people don't realize is that it usually takes a significant amount of time and work before you start making good money from your side hustle.

Success happens over the long haul, not overnight. If you want your side hustle to be truly profitable, you need to be willing to make sacrifices again and again until you've finally reached your objective.

World famous soccer player Pele said:

> *Success is no accident. It is hard work, perseverance, learning, studying, sacrifice and most of all, love of what you are doing or learning to do.*

If you want to succeed, you must be willing to work hard and persevere. The good news is that if you persevere, you almost certainly will succeed.

All that being said, you must be confident that you can do it. If you're constantly doubting yourself, you'll have a hard time getting traction. But if you have faith in yourself and believe firmly in your abilities, you truly can achieve great things.

The best time to start a side hustle is right now. Don't wait any longer. There will never be a *perfect* time to get started. Start working on your project today and simply adjust as time goes on.

> **Start where you are.
> Use what you have.
> Do what you can.**
>
> Arthur Ashe

Identify Your Passions and Interests

So how do you identify *what* your side hustle should be? How do you know what you should give your time to? How can you determine the best activities to focus on?

You start by identifying the things you're most passionate about and interested in.

See, a side hustle is the intersection of passion and profit. In other words, it's all about taking the things you love and are good at and turning them into a profitable gig.

So, the first step is to identify what you love to do AND are good at doing.
Both elements are required. If you want your side hustle to be sustainable, you must love doing it. If you don't, you'll burn out quickly. When hard work and sacrifices are needed, you won't want to. A successful side hustle involves an activity that you love doing.

You must also be *good* at your side hustle. In other words, you must have the necessary skill set to make it a reality. If you're not good at creating your product or performing your service, others simply won't want to pay you for it.

Ask yourself these questions:

- What do you absolutely love doing?
- What have people told you that you're good at?
- What do you lose track of time doing?
- What valuable skills do you have that people would pay for?
- What needs can you meet?

These questions will help you find the intersection of passion and profit. They'll help you determine both your skillset and what you love. When these two things combine, you have a viable side hustle.

There is a psychological concept called "flow." It's when you find yourself so immersed in an activity that you lose all track of time and are simply focused on what's in front of you. Your mind isn't distracted at all. Rather, you simply "flow" with your activity.

When do you find yourself in the "flow" of things? Pay attention to these moments. It's these activities that could turn into viable side hustles.

"

The biggest adventure you can take is to live the life of your dreams.

Oprah Winfrey

Validate Your Side Hustle

Once you've determined what you think your side hustle should be, it's important to validate it. In other words, be able to demonstrate that people will really pay you for what you offer them. Determine if there's a "market need" for the product or services that you will offer.

After all, it won't do you any good to start your side hustle, only to discover that no one actually wants what you're offering. You'll end up spending hours and hours on things that won't generate any extra income. You'll also become discouraged and probably want to give up.

Therefore, it's essential to ensure that people will want what you have to offer, even if it's just a few people.

So how can you do that? Where can you find an audience on which to test out your idea?

Some simple ideas include:

- Ask your friends on social media if they would be interested in what you have to offer.

- If you have an email list, send out a poll to them, asking who would be interested in what you're going to offer.

- Create a sign-up list where people can get more information. If numerous people sign up, it's a sign that your idea has legs.

- Offer to let people pre-purchase your offer. If a number of people purchase from you, you know that you're onto something good.

Your goal is to avoid wasting time on ideas that won't get any traction. If your polls, emails, and sign-up list aren't getting much of a response, it may be time to move on to a different side hustle.

It's really important that you not get discouraged at this point. If you can't get any traction on your side hustle, that doesn't mean you have to give it up altogether. It simply means you may not be able to make a sustainable income from it. Or, you may simply need to adjust your approach to your product.

There are dozens of ways to make money, and you can certainly find a side hustle that allows you to do what you love.

> **Dreams come true. Without that possibility, nature would not incite us to have them.**
>
> John Updike

Determine What Sets You Apart From Your Competitors

Unless you're building something completely new and revolutionary, you're going to be competing against others. Whether you're selling a widget or offering coaching services, there are going to be others against whom you're competing for business.

If you're going to succeed with your side hustle, you need to find a way to differentiate yourself from your competitors. In other words, figure out how you're going to stand out from the crowd. How you're going to attract customers. How your offer is different from what others are offering.

How can you differentiate yourself from your competitors? There are numerous ways, including:

- Better quality products or services

- Better customer service
- Faster delivery
- Less expensive products or services
- Aggressive sales tactics
- Higher or lower profit margins
- A noble cause that you support with profits from your product

For example, let's say you're selling soap online. You could create a unique soap that is better quality than most other soap out there. Because your soap is better quality, you can sell it for a higher price and make higher profit margins.

Or you could sell your soap at a discount and sell a higher volume of soap. Or you could create an aggressive online marketing campaign where you're trying to get your soap in front of more eyeballs than anyone else.

If you don't find a way to differentiate yourself from your competitors, there's no reason that customers should purchase from you. You absolutely must find a way to stand out in the crowd.

> **Commitment leads to action. Action brings your dream closer.**
>
> **Marcia Wieder**

Define Your Goals

Once you've determined what your side hustle will be, have validated that idea, and determined how you'll stand out from the crowd, it's time to define your overall goals. Defining clear goals will help you know what steps you need to take in order to turn your hustle into a reality.

Consider laying out a set of goals that sequentially follow one another.

For example, if you're going to sell products on eBay, your first goal may be to create an eBay account. Your second goal may be to research the products that sell best on eBay. Your third goal may be to source the products to sell and your fourth goal may be to list those products.

When setting your goals, ensure that they are realistic. Your goal is to get traction, not reach your end goal right off the bat. Setting a goal of selling 1,000 bars of soap is a great goal, but there are probably a dozen smaller goals that need to be achieved before you can reach your final goal.

Each goal should be realistic and achievable. If your goals aren't realistic, you'll again find yourself getting discouraged when you don't meet those goals. The more discouraged you get, the more inclined you'll be to give up your side hustle.

So what are some small goals you can set that will give you traction on your hustle? These small goals should all contribute to your big, overall goal.

Do you need to...

- Research your market?
- Research the desires of your ideal customer?
- Create a website?
- Send out an email to your list, letting them know about your offer?

Start taking small steps that will lead you to your overall goal. Try to set goals that will move you forward on a daily, weekly, and monthly basis.

> **The only boundaries for me are those I place on myself.**
>
> Shelly Wu

Create Milestones

One of the great temptations with a side hustle is to put off actually launching. You can get so caught up in trying to make things perfect that you never actually get your side hustle off the ground.

Eventually, you just need to get started. Yes, you need to reach the small goals that will lead you to your big goal, but eventually, you just need to get your idea out into the wild and evaluate the response.

Side hustles are iterative. In other words, you launch, refine, fix problems, and then keep going. With each iteration, your side hustle gets better and better. The more iterations you do, the more highly refined your hustle becomes and the more revenue you generate.

In order to launch, set milestones that will force you to take action. Setting milestones for yourself will ensure that you actually take action and don't delay. Each milestone should be tied directly to a date.

For example, let's say you're launching a coaching program. Your first milestone might be to create your website within the next month. Your next milestone might be to send out an email to all the potential clients you know. Your third milestone might be to advertise your coaching practice on Facebook.

Think of it this way: Milestones equal movement. When you set milestones for yourself, it forces you to move forward and prevents you from trying to get everything perfect.

Like your goals, your milestones should also be realistic and achievable. For example, it's probably not realistic to think that you can get a website designed in a day (unless you're an amazing web designer). Give yourself a reasonable amount of time to achieve your milestone.

The more you reach your milestones, the more encouraged you'll be about your side hustle. The more encouraged you are, the more you'll want to reach more milestones, which will keep your project moving at a rapid pace. Avoid making excuses when it comes to meeting your milestones. Hold yourself to deadlines, and if you need to get friends to hold you accountable, don't hesitate to do that.

> First say to yourself what you would be; and then do what you have to do.

Epictetus

Determine How You Will Sell

Before you can launch your side hustle, you'll need to determine *how* you're going to sell your product or service.

Thankfully, there are dozens of ways to sell products and services, such as:

1. You can always sell in person.

    - If you're selling a product, you can take it to trade shows and markets.

    - You could even go from door to door if you have the courage.

    - You can sell directly to your friends or host parties where you show off your product.

    - You can meet one-on-one with potential customers and tell them about the benefits of the service you offer.

2. You can also sell just about any product or service online as well.

- For example, if your product is crafty (like soap), artisan, or vintage you can sell on Etsy.

- If you're getting products from thrift shops, you can sell them on eBay or Poshmark.

- If you're trying to break into the freelance world, you can find jobs in dozens of industries on websites like Upwork, Fiverr, or Thumbtack.

- If you're selling eBooks, you can list them on Amazon.

- If you're promoting a course you've created, you can sell it through Kajabi, Teachable, Udemy, or Thinkific.

- If you're a handyman, you can find hundreds of jobs on TaskRabbit.

- If you're a coach, you can use Tailored.coach to connect with your clients.

- And, of course, you can build your own website - your business 'home on the web.

No matter what you're selling, there is an online platform to sell it. A simple way to find the platform that's best for you is to Google "Sell [PRODUCT/SERVICE] online". This will bring up dozens of results and allow you to find the best place to sell your product or service.

> **I have accepted fear as a part of life - specifically the fear of change.**
>
> **I have gone ahead despite the pounding in the heart that says: turn back.**
>
> Erica Jong

Start Selling

This point is short and sweet. Once you've done the initial work up front, you simply need to get started.

Your side hustle will *not* be perfect when you first launch it. You'll make mistakes. You may have trouble landing your first customers. Regardless, at some point, you must launch your side hustle if you want to make any money from it.

As noted above, building a successful side hustle involves a lot of tweaking, refining, and making changes on the fly. If you try to get everything perfect before you launch, you'll never get started.

In the initial launch phase, it may take some time for you to gain significant traction. You'll have to work hard to promote yourself. But it's worth the work. If your side hustle is valuable, people will eventually buy into it.

Avoid getting discouraged if you don't have massive success right off the bat. Keep working, refining, promoting, and selling. Eventually, you'll hit on the right combination and the customers will start coming.

> **Figure out what your purpose is in life, what you really and truly want to do with your time and your life; then be willing to sacrifice everything and then some to achieve it.**
>
> Quintina Ragnacci

Market Yourself

To make your side hustle as successful as possible, it's essential to consistently market yourself. You'll need to promote your hustle, so it gets in front of as many people as possible.

Don't be modest on this point. If you truly believe in what you're doing, then go for it with all your might. Market yourself hard and relentlessly.

What are some effective ways to market your side hustle?

- Ask your friends and family to spread the word.
- Hand out flyers telling others about what you offer.
- Give out free samples (if you're selling a product).
- Tell people about it on social media.
- Build an email list and regularly promote your product or service to the list.
- Start a blog and consistently talk about pain points your customers feel.

- Create a YouTube channel specifically dedicated to giving loads of value to potential customers.
- Start a podcast in which you talk about elements of your industry and business.
- Appear as a guest on other's podcasts.
- Do webinars where you teach valuable lessons and then promote your product or service at the end.
- Use paid advertising to drive people to your website.
- Consistently apply for jobs on the platforms mentioned above.

Generally speaking, the more value you can give potential customers for *free*, the more likely they are to pay for your product or services.

For example, let's say you're a health and fitness coach. You could create a YouTube channel in which you teach people exercises and workout routines. This is giving free value to people.

The more you do this, the more people will see that you're an expert in your field and the more they'll want to hire you as their health and fitness coach.

Again, don't be afraid to market yourself. You've put in hours of hard work to get to this point. You've created a product or service that you truly believe in. You know that you truly can help people and really want to make a difference in the world.

So, try to get yourself in front of as many people as possible. Don't worry about what others will think. If you want to succeed with your side hustle, you must market yourself constantly.

> **Vision without action is merely a dream. Action without vision just passes the time. Vision with action can change the world.**
>
> **Joel Barker**

Get Feedback From Your Customers

After you've launched, keep improving. If you want to achieve the kind of success that will change your life, you need to constantly better the product or service that you're offering.

After all, some people will buy an okay product or service. A LOT of people will buy an outstanding product or service.

This is where customer feedback is invaluable. Your customers can honestly tell you what is and what isn't working. They can help you see past your blind spots and identify areas for change that you never would have seen on your own.

So, ask your customers these important questions:

- What do they like about your product or service?

- What features do they find most valuable and which ones could use improvement?

- How has your product or service benefited them and what benefits would they still like to see?

- Which pain points could you more effectively solve?

- What features could you add that would make your offer even more valuable to your customers?

- How can you create the absolute best experience for those who have bought into what you're selling?

Asking customers for feedback is a way of being transparent and authentic with your customers. It shows them that you really care about them and their opinion and that you want to offer them the best possible product or service possible.

The more authentic you are with your customers, the more they'll support you over the long run. As they see how dedicated you are to constant improvement, they'll want to continue working with you and using your product or service.

> **Chase the vision, not the money. The money will end up following you.**
>
> ## Tony Hsieh

Provide Amazing Experiences For Your Customers

One of the best ways to get new customers and keep your existing customers is to create amazing experiences for them. These experiences don't need to be anything crazy.

Your goal is to show them that you care deeply about them and want them to be incredibly happy with what you have to offer.

How can you create incredible experiences for your customers?

There are literally dozens of simple ways:

- Provide amazing customer support
- Send a handwritten thank you note with every product
- Include an extra surprise with your product
- Dedicate extended time to helping your clients work through their challenges
- Send a card on the anniversary of their first purchase
- Create short, custom videos thanking each one of your clients or customers

- Call each customer just to say thank you

The list goes on and on. The goal is simply to make your customers feel special. You want them to feel like they really matter to you and aren't simply a way for you to make money.

The more you can delight and surprise your customers, the more likely it is that they'll tell their friends and colleagues about you, which will generate referral business. If you really go over the top with the way you treat your customers, you may even get exposure in prominent publications.

But ultimately, it's not about getting referral business or big exposure, although those things are certainly valuable. It's about treating your customers like real people who you actually care about.

> **The only thing worse than starting something and failing...is not starting something.**
>
> **Seth Godin**

Build Sustainable Cash Flow

Eventually, if all things go well (and they will!), there will come a point where you have to decide whether or not you want to quit your day job and make your side hustle your full-time job.

Isn't that exciting to think about? You really could turn your passion project into a full-time, income producing job!

So how do you do that?

The final step is to get to the point where you have sustainable cash flow. In other words, you need to have a relatively stable amount of money coming in every month. If you have consistent cash flow, this gives you the option of quitting your day job.

How much sustainable cash flow should you have? Ideally, you want your side hustle to be generating at least 75% of your income. This will give you the flexibility to decide whether or not you want to quit your day job.

When thinking about your income, remember to take into account expenses. You'll have to pay self-employment tax at the end of the year. You also probably have expenses involved in keeping your side hustle up and running. Take all these things into account when deciding whether to make the plunge.

One important thing to note when it comes to quitting your day job. There will probably be a sense of fear and apprehension around quitting your job. After all, your job offers you stability.

Avoid allowing fear to keep you from following your dreams.

Fear is a big dream killer. If you've gotten your side hustle to the point where you're generating significant income, then it's time to seriously consider whether or not you should focus on doing it full time.

And consider this. If you're only doing your side hustle part time *and* you're making enough money to consider quitting your day job, think about how much more you could make if you were doing it full-time! Going full-time with your side hustle could actually produce significantly more income for you.

When that time comes, ask yourself, *"What is keeping me from taking the leap? What is keeping me from pursuing my dream full-time?"*

If the answer is fear, that might be a signal that it's actually time to go all-in on your side hustle.

"
I don't focus on what I'm up against. I focus on my goals and I try to ignore the rest.

Venus Williams

Side Hustle Your Way To Freedom

The beauty of the side hustle is that, when done properly, it can create freedom for you. If you're working a day job, it can give you additional income that can set you up for financial freedom. If you're not working a full-time job (like a stay-at-home mom), a side hustle can provide valuable income to your family.

And eventually, you may be able to take your passion and turn it into a full-time job. That's the real power of the side hustle!

Over the course of this book, you've learned a lot!

We talked about:

- Preparing yourself for the hard work of the side hustle
- Identifying your passions, desires, and skills
- Validating your side hustle

- Defining the goals that you want to achieve
- Creating milestones that will keep your side hustle moving
- Determining how you'll sell your side hustle products or services
- Starting the actual process of selling
- Marketing yourself effectively
- Getting feedback from your customers
- Providing amazing customer experiences
- Building sustainable cash flow

You now know what you need to do in order to start making money with your side hustle. You even know what you need to do in order to transform your side hustle into a full-time job.

The only question now is, "What's stopping you?"

Nothing is holding you back from getting your side hustle up and running.

So, don't wait any longer. Get hustling!

EXCLUSIVE OFFER

You took action to take control of your income and future, and for that I want to give you an exclusive offer only available to those who purchase this book.

There is much work ahead to get your business launched, and I want to help you get there.

That is why I developed the Passion to Profit Action Guide, a step-by-step training course to help you get started profiting from your passion.

Below is a coupon code for you to get 50% off this training.

BONUS: When you purchase the training using the code below, you will also receive a complimentary coaching call where I will help you set goals and milestones to ensure your success.

Register at: getmindmagnet.com/register/p2p

Use Code: p2pbook

www.ingramcontent.com/pod-product-compliance
Lightning Source LLC
Chambersburg PA
CBHW070801050426
42452CB00012B/2449